EMOTIONAL HEALTH ISSUES

Stress and Depression

By Jane Bingham

Health Consultant: John G. Samanich, M.D.

 Gareth Stevens
Publishing

A WEEKLY READER COMPANY

**Please visit our web site at
www.garethstevens.com.**
**For a free color catalog describing Gareth Stevens
Publishing's list of high-quality books, call
1-800-542-2595 (USA) or 1-800-387-3178 (Canada).
Gareth Stevens Publishing's fax: 1-877-542-2596**

Library of Congress Cataloging in Publication Data
Bingham, Jane.
  Stress and depression / Jane Bingham. — North American ed.
    p. cm. — (Emotional health issues)
  Originally published: London : Wayland, 2008.
  Includes bibliographical references and index.
  ISBN-10: 0-8368-9203-8 (lib. bdg.)
  ISBN-13: 978-0-8368-9203-1 (lib. bdg.)
  1. Stress in adolescence—Juvenile literature.
  2. Depression in adolescence—Juvenile literature.
  I. Title.
RJ506.D4B48   2009
618.92'8527—dc22   2008005237

The information in this book is not intended to substitute for professional medical or psychological care. The case studies are based on real experiences, but the names are fictitious. All people in the photos are models except where a caption specifically names an individual.

This North American edition first published in 2009 by
Gareth Stevens Publishing
A Weekly Reader® Company
1 Reader's Digest Road
Pleasantville, NY 10570-7000 USA

This U.S. edition copyright © 2009 by Gareth Stevens, Inc.
Original edition copyright © 2008 by Wayland. First published in Great Britain in 2008
by Wayland, 338 Euston Road, London NW1 3BH, United Kingdom.

Series Editor: Nicola Edwards   Consultant: Peter Evans
Designer: Alix Wood   Picture Researcher: Kathy Lockley

Gareth Stevens Managing Editor: Lisa M. Herrington
Gareth Stevens Senior Editor: Barbara Bakowski
Gareth Stevens Creative Director: Lisa Donovan

Photo credits: Liam Bailey/Photofusion: 5; Paul Baldesare/Photofusion: 11, 26; Heide
Benser/zefa/Corbis: 7; Bubbles Photolibrary/Alamy Images: 10, 24; Jacky Chapman/Photofusion: 42;
Mary-Kate Denny/Alamy Images: 40; Kevin Dodge/Corbis: 29; Raymond Gehman/Corbis: 23; Gina
Glover/Photofusion: 14; Crispin Hughes/Photofusion: 12; Jupiterimages/Brand X/Alamy Images: 6, Cover;
Image100/Corbis: 25; Image Source/Corbis: 16, 20, 37; Leblond/Stockphoto/Alamy Images: 45; Roy
McMahon/Corbis: 30; Mika/zefa/Corbis: 32; Mira/Alamy Images: 33; Roy Morsch/Corbis: 31; Gabe
Palmer/Corbis: 28; Helene Rogers/Alamy Images: 22; Shoot/zefa/Corbis: 43; Ariel Skelley/Corbis: 9;
Christa Stadtler/Photofusion: title page, 36; Tom Stewart/Corbis: 33; Wayland Archive: 4; Wishlist: 8, 17, 18,
19, 21, 34, 38, 41

Printed in China
1 2 3 4 5 6 7 8 9 10 09 08

Contents

Words that appear in **boldface** type are in the glossary on page 46.

Introduction

Over the past year, Sam has had to cope with a lot of **stress**, and now it's really getting him down. He feels exhausted all the time, no matter how long he sleeps. He just wants to stay in bed and not get up again. He can't face doing anything—not even going out with his friends. When he thinks of the future, he just sees emptiness. Sam has felt sad before but never as he does now. He feels completely cut off from his family and friends, and they don't know what they can do to help him.

Sam is experiencing **depression**. All the stresses in his life have combined to make him ill. Depression is an overwhelming sense of sadness and despair. It can take over people's lives and leave them unable to cope with the demands of everyday living. Teenagers who have depression can't just "shake it off." They need support to help them recover.

Many cases of depression are triggered by stress. Depression can be caused by distressing events, such as the death of a loved one or a major life change. As young people enter their teenage years, they encounter a lot of new stresses. Sometimes all these pressures can be very hard to handle.

Being depressed can make young people feel isolated, but they shouldn't have to cope with their feelings alone.

Depression is not uncommon in the teenage years. Teens from all backgrounds can experience stress and depression.

Find out more

This book gives you the facts about depression. It describes the impact that the illness can have on people's lives and examines the various causes of stress that can lead to depression. Finally, it shows how people can recover from depression, and suggests ways to cope with stress.

Too much stress

No one can avoid stress and pressure. In fact, sometimes pressure can have a positive effect. Many teenagers enjoy the challenge of being under pressure in a sports match or an academic competition. When stress builds up, though, it is natural for people to feel anxious. Teens who experience a combination of stress and **anxiety** may be vulnerable to becoming depressed.

It's a fact: depression

- About one in eight teenagers will experience depression before reaching adulthood.

- Episodes of depression in teenagers generally last about eight months.

- About 5 percent of teenagers experience serious, long-term depression.

Chapter 1: *What is depression?*

People often say they are "depressed" when they are feeling sad or down. But true depression is different from simply having a bad day or feeling down. Major depression is a serious **mental illness**.

Not just a passing mood

All people have times when they feel low—especially when sad things happen—but usually those feelings don't take over their lives. After a few days or weeks of feeling down, most people manage to get on with everyday activities again. Although they may occasionally feel sad, they know that they can look forward to a future when they will feel better again.

When people experience depression, their feelings of sadness just don't go away. Depression can last for weeks or months, and, in very severe cases, even for years. People who are depressed can't escape from their negative thoughts, and they can't imagine a time when they will feel better.

When teens are depressed, they may have trouble concentrating on schoolwork. If they fall behind in their studies, stress and anxiety can increase.

Sadness and despair

Teenagers with depression describe their powerful feelings of sadness and despair. Some of them talk about looking into an endless black hole, and some experience the frightening sensation of being stuck, with no way out. Some very depressed people decide that they can't go on living and attempt suicide.

Tired all the time

A common symptom of depression is **fatigue**, or an overwhelming sense of tiredness. Many people who are depressed sleep for hours on end, hardly emerging from their bedrooms at all. They lack energy and may spend many hours sitting in a chair, simply staring into space.

The feeling of exhaustion that often accompanies depression can lead people to drop out of social activities. Some teenagers with depression skip school frequently and find it hard to keep up with schoolwork, clubs, and sports.

In focus: altered sleep patterns

Depression often affects people's sleep patterns. Some people with depression sleep for very long stretches; others sleep much less than they did before. It is very common for people suffering from depression to wake up early and then be unable to go back to sleep. Depressed people sometimes experience **insomnia**, when they struggle to get to sleep or they wake during the night.

Teens with depression often struggle to get up in the morning. Then they battle with feelings of tiredness throughout the day.

Many teens with depression feel angry and misunderstood. Instead of being able to turn to their families for help, they feel cut off and isolated.

In focus: aches and pains

Young people who are depressed frequently experience headaches or stomachaches. Many say their arms and legs feel heavy and achy.

In some cases, the family and friends of depressed teens become impatient with their physical complaints because there is no obvious medical cause for the aches and pains. The painful sensations that a depressed person feels are real, however, and they are often clear symptoms of mental distress.

Anxious and distracted

Many people with depression experience powerful feelings of anxiety. They may become agitated for no apparent reason, pacing restlessly around the room. They may also feel distracted and have trouble concentrating. It is common for people who are depressed to become much more forgetful than before. They may have great difficulty making simple, everyday decisions.

Feeling angry or guilty

Depression makes some people feel irritable, angry, and hostile. They describe a sense of pent-up rage and frustration. Their angry feelings can make them lash out at their friends and families. They may be critical, sarcastic, or abusive.

Depression can also make teens especially sensitive to criticism, rejection, or perceived failure. Teenagers who are depressed may feel as though they are worthless. They sometimes blame themselves for negative events or circumstances.

Alone and apart

Many teenagers with depression describe their intense feelings of isolation. Just when they are most in need of help, they withdraw from others and become harder to reach than before. They are sometimes told to "snap out of it" by people who do not understand what they are experiencing. That reaction can deepen their sense of isolation. Many young people who are depressed lose interest in social activities and put up barriers by becoming moody and irritable. As a result, they feel that they are forced to struggle with their problems alone. As their depression becomes more severe, teenagers may retreat further from family life and from their social life with friends. They may spend long periods of time alone and may even run away from home.

Taking risks

Sometimes, being depressed can drive people to take serious risks. Depressed teenagers may start abusing drugs or drinking large amounts of alcohol. They may shoplift, drive recklessly, or engage in unsafe sexual practices. Their risky behavior is a sign that they are feeling desperate. Without any hope for the future, they simply don't care what happens to them. High-risk behavior can also be a cry for help from some teens.

Teenagers and their parents or caregivers sometimes find themselves in conflict with one another. Relationships within a family can be improved if members communicate openly about disagreements.

Feeling worthless

People who are depressed usually have very low **self-esteem**. They feel that they are worthless and that their lives don't matter. When teenagers become depressed, they may neglect their appearance. Sometimes they stop taking showers and changing their clothes regularly.

Some teens express feelings of despair by engaging in cutting or other forms of self-harm. Any form of self-harm should be taken very seriously.

Some people with depression have strong feelings of self-loathing and guilt. They may believe that they are a burden to their families and others. Sometimes they attempt to deal with their overwhelming negative feelings by engaging in cutting or other forms of **self-harm**.

Self-harm

Many people who self-harm cut themselves with razor blades or burn their skin with lighters or cigarettes. Self-harm is a physical expression of inner pain and an attempt to relieve emotional pressure. It should also be seen as a cry for help. When teenagers harm themselves, they are sending out a clear message of pain and despair.

Changed eating patterns

People who are depressed typically experience changes in their eating patterns. They may express too much or too little interest in eating and have a large weight gain or loss.

Some depressed teenagers restrict their food intake severely in an attempt to change themselves and take control of their lives. Others turn to food for comfort and eat even when they are not hungry. They may develop an **eating disorder**.

Some people who are depressed **binge**, or eat unusually large amounts of food quickly, and then feel terrible

All families have arguments, but serious family conflict can trigger depression.

afterward. Following binges, they may **purge** their bodies of food by deliberately vomiting or by using **laxatives**.

Abnormal eating patterns can be signs of serious eating disorders, including **anorexia nervosa**, **bulimia nervosa**, and **compulsive eating disorder**. Eating disorders frequently occur with other mental health problems such as anxiety and depression. It remains unclear whether eating disorders trigger depression or whether people who are depressed are more likely to develop eating disorders.

CASE STUDY

Max had been having a hard time at home, frequently arguing with his stepdad. Sometimes Max felt so helpless and angry that he punched his bedroom door until his fists bled. At school he got into fights and became involved with a crowd of kids who shoplifted for thrills. Max liked the excitement of taking risks because it distracted him from his feelings of sadness and anger. Afterward, though, he felt worse than before. Fortunately, Max's teacher realized that there was something more behind the teen's changes in behavior. She recognized that Max might be depressed.

Some teenagers with depression withdraw into their rooms and may even stay in bed all day.

Thoughts of death

When people have severe depression, they may start to think a lot about death. Depressed teenagers sometimes read poetry about death or listen to music with morbid themes. They may start to give away their possessions. These kinds of behaviors signal that a person is thinking seriously about death, and the warning signs should not be ignored. When someone is experiencing major depression, suicide can be a real possibility.

Suicide and suicide attempts

Depression sometimes causes feelings of despair so overwhelming that thoughts of suicide take over. Teenagers who are depressed for long periods may begin to see death as something to be desired. If they do not share their feelings, they may commit suicide.

Some people who talk about suicide do not truly wish to die. They may threaten to kill themselves or even attempt to commit suicide, but they also make arrangements to be discovered before it is too late. These people are reaching out for help by revealing their desperate feelings. Anyone who threatens or attempts to commit suicide is in urgent need of expert medical help. All suicide attempts should be taken seriously.

Suicide helplines

When teenagers feel suicidal, they need help fast. They can call helplines that are available 24 hours a day and are staffed by trained, experienced **counselors**. Most counselors talk to teenagers in complete privacy and confidence. They offer support but do not judge or blame. Counselors can direct troubled teens to organizations and people who can help. (See page 47 for a list of helplines.)

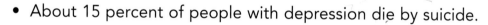

It's a fact: suicide

- About 15 percent of people with depression die by suicide.

- In the United States, suicide is the third leading cause of death among teenagers.

- In a recent survey of high school students, the National Youth Violence Prevention Resource Center found that almost one in five teens had thought about suicide in the previous year. Approximately one in six teens had made plans for suicide, and more than one in 12 teens had attempted suicide.

- Girls are more likely to attempt suicide, but boys are more than twice as likely to die by completed suicide.

Chemical changes

Medical experts think some types of depression are mainly triggered by chemical changes in the brain. Both **seasonal affective disorder (SAD)** and **bipolar disorder** are types of depression that are caused by recognizable changes in the chemistry of the brain.

Seasonal affective disorder

Some people living in northern countries suffer from depression during the winter months. As the days get shorter and the hours of sunlight diminish, people with SAD become depressed. Symptoms include sadness, irritability, changes in sleeping and eating, poor concentration, fatigue, aches and pains, and severe anxiety. The symptoms go away in the spring.

Researchers have discovered that a lack of sunlight affects the chemistry of the brain, and in some people the lack of light triggers depression. The most effective treatment for people with SAD is light therapy for one to two hours a day. Special light boxes

Some people respond to a lack of sunlight by becoming seriously depressed. They have a condition known as seasonal affective disorder, or SAD.

with high-intensity fluorescent tubes can be installed in homes to help lessen feelings of depression.

Bipolar disorder

A very small proportion of the population has bipolar disorder, also known as **manic** depression. People with bipolar disorder experience periods of depression alternating with times when they are very happy and excited, or manic.

Bipolar disorder usually develops when people are in their late teens or early twenties. Some people with bipolar disorder experience dramatic mood swings throughout their lives. Others have just a few episodes. Between 20 and 40 percent of young people who have depression later develop bipolar disorder, according to a report by the surgeon general of the United States.

People with bipolar disorder need expert treatment to control their mood swings. Treatment usually includes a combination of **psychotherapy** and prescribed mood-stabilizing medication, such as **lithium**.

Chapter 2: *Under pressure*

The suicide rate among young people rose in recent years, based on the latest numbers available from the U.S. Centers for Disease Control and Prevention. From 2003 to 2004, the suicide rate among people ages 10 to 24 saw the largest single-year increase since 1990. While that increase may be a temporary spike, it could suggest a troubling reversal in earlier trends. One cause might be a rise in depression among teens and preteens. Some experts say the stresses of modern teenage life put members of this age-group under a lot of pressure—at home, at school, and among their peers. All of these stresses can leave young people feeling anxious and helpless.

Pressures at home

When children enter their teens, life at home becomes more complicated than before. As teenagers struggle to gain their independence, they come into conflict with their parents or caregivers. While family conflicts are normal, they can be stressful. Some teens become angry and distressed. Others withdraw from family life and spend a lot of time alone.

If the family conflict continues for a long time, a negative atmosphere can

It is common for teenagers and their parents to disagree, but arguments can become a serious cause of tension in a household.

After a family breakup, young people can be faced with difficult and painful situations. The birth of a half-sibling, for example, can make a teen feel left out.

build up. In this situation, some teens feel lonely and despairing. Others struggle to cope with pent-up anger and frustration, which can lead to depression.

Family breakup

By the time children reach their teens, a lot of them have experienced a family breakup. Many children go through their parents' divorce with few problems or long-term negative effects. For other children, however, the effects of divorce can be traumatic and long-lived. Teenagers may be especially sensitive to family problems and may feel pressure to intervene in the conflict. They also have to deal with the consequences, such as missing one of their parents or coping with a stepfamily. It is not surprising

CASE STUDY

When Amy was young, she had a happy family life. By the time she was 13, however, life at home had changed. Her parents argued a lot, and both of them were sad and withdrawn. Amy tried her best to make things better, but nothing worked; in the end, her parents decided to divorce. After the breakup, Amy and her sister lived mostly with their mother. Their dad remarried and moved in with his new wife and her young sons. In this new situation, Amy felt worried about her mom, who was lonely and angry. Amy also had to get used to a different way of life with her dad and his new family. Amy felt stressed about all the changes in her life, and she missed the times when her family was still together. She struggled to cope for as long as she could, but eventually she was overwhelmed by feelings of depression.

that family breakups sometimes contribute to depression in young people, particularly if divorces take place in an atmosphere of bitterness and anger.

Reacting to a split

Before a divorce, most families go through a painful period of conflict. Teens may be upset when their parents argue and feel sad. Some children try to intervene, and they often get hurt in the process. Other young people decide to withdraw, which can leave them feeling miserable and alone.

Teenagers usually experience a mixture of emotions when their parents split up. They feel sadness as well as anger about what they've lost. Their loyalties may be divided between their parents.

Many teens mistakenly feel guilt about their parents' breakup. Most of all, the young people feel helpless as they watch the world they know fall apart. These reactions can cause depression as teenagers become overwhelmed by their negative feelings.

A new way of life

After a couple has split up, their children's lives can change significantly—and quickly. Teenagers may have to adjust to new living arrangements.

Some children must divide their time between two homes or move to a new home and attend a different school. These disruptions can be especially difficult and stressful for teenagers, who want a social life of their own.

Listening to their parents' arguments can be distressing for teens. Faced with this situation, many young people feel helpless and depressed.

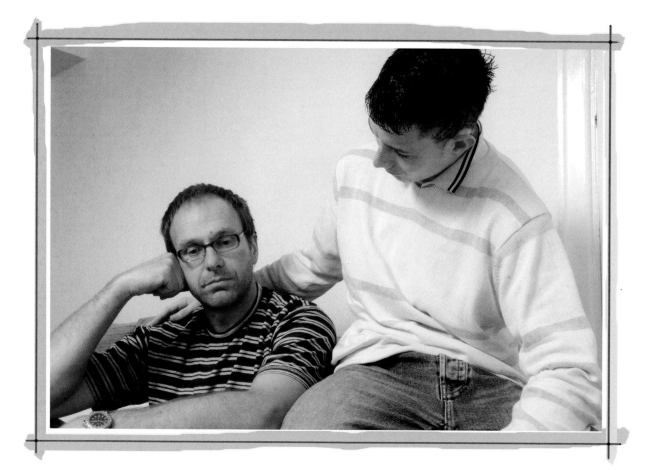

Some teenagers have to cope with their parents' feelings of despair. This can be a difficult burden to bear at a time when the teens are feeling unhappy, too.

Children who live with just one parent often miss the other parent badly. Teens may struggle with powerful feelings of sadness, anger, and blame. They may also feel responsible and anxious for the newly single parent.

If divorced parents are depressed and angry, their kids can experience negative effects. The children's feelings of anxiety may be heightened.

In focus: *guilty feelings*

It is common for teenagers to experience feelings of guilt when their parents divorce. Children may believe that their behavior has somehow caused the problem between their parents. These feelings of guilt are natural but mistaken. Some teens feel embarrassed or awkward about their parents' breakup. They may worry about what their friends or other people think. Unless teenagers talk about their emotions, these negative feelings can lead to depression.

Some children experience difficulties when their parents take a new partner. Many teenagers struggle to get used to the presence of a new adult in their lives.

Changing families

In many cases, the children of divorced parents have to get used to a lot of new people in their lives. Their parents may have new partners, and these partners may have children of their own. Changes in the family's structure can be very stressful.

You're not my parent!

Coping with a parent's new partner can be especially hard for a teenager. Even if the teenager likes the new adult, he or she may resent the newcomer for taking the biological parent's place. A young person may find it difficult to have a new adult making the household rules. In addition, a teen may feel uncomfortable about a parent's new relationship at a time when the teen is discovering his or her own sexuality.

Blended families

Today, many teenagers live in "blended" families. Some teens have stepbrothers and stepsisters; some have half-brothers and half-sisters; and others have both. If both parents have remarried, children can belong to two blended families. While blended families can offer great opportunities for fun, they can also be a source of conflict and unhappiness.

Teenagers sometimes experience strong feelings of resentment toward their stepbrothers and stepsisters. They may feel squeezed out of their old position in the family. They may resent having to share their parent with new children, and they may object to any intrusion into their private space. Faced with new family members whom they dislike, some teens may become hostile. Others cut themselves off from the rest of the family, becoming isolated and lonely.

The arrival of a new half-sibling can help bring a family together. Sometimes, though, a baby can make the older children feel left out. Some teens say they feel less loved than before because their parents seem to give all their attention to the new child. In this situation, parents sometimes are unaware that their teenagers have become depressed.

Having to share personal space with stepsiblings can leave young people feeling angry and depressed— especially when nobody seems to understand their feelings.

It's a fact: divorce and remarriage

- Each year, more than a million children under the age of 18 experience their parents' divorce.

- Today, at least one-third of all children in the United States are expected to live in a stepfamily before they reach age 18.

- Recent research suggests that children from the ages of 10 to 14 may have the most difficult time adjusting to a stepfamily. Overall, boys appear to accept a stepfamily more quickly than girls do.

Pressures at school

For many teenagers, school can be a very stressful place. Students feel pressure to earn good grades, perform well in sports and other extracurricular activities, and get along with their peers. Some teenagers seem able to take challenges in stride, but others feel weighed down by the need to succeed.

Being the best

Some schools set high standards, and competition among students may be fierce, both to gain admission to the school and to do well once they are there. Their parents may expect great accomplishments from them, and children may be anxious about letting their families down.

Many pupils also have very high expectations of themselves and blame themselves bitterly if they fail. These conscientious perfectionists often study for long hours and become excessively worried and anxious about their performance on exams.

Some teens have to juggle after-school jobs with a heavy homework load. They can feel overwhelmed with exhaustion and become depressed. Students who live at boarding schools sometimes have to cope with feelings of homesickness and loneliness.

Many students feel pressure to do well at school and on tests. Sometimes the burden of stress is a factor in the development of depression.

Teenagers who aim for success in sports often experience pressure. If they fail to reach their goals, they can become severely depressed.

Teenagers can feel driven to succeed in areas besides schoolwork, such as sports, music, and dance. Some young athletes experience great pressure—from their coaches, their schoolmates, their parents, and themselves—to perform at their best on the day of a big game or competition.

Exam stress

While most people don't enjoy taking exams, some young people find the experience unbearably stressful. These anxious teenagers have trouble eating and sleeping in the days and weeks before a big test. They may be physically sick before the exam or feel paralyzed with nervousness. Their anxiety can negatively affect their performance. Young people who regularly experience overwhelming exam anxiety should seek expert help. An extreme reaction to tests can be a sign of deeper, underlying anxieties and problems.

In focus: not smart to look smart?

Some teenagers feel under a lot of pressure *not* to do well at school, even though they want to. They may think it isn't "cool" to work hard and earn good grades. Students may believe that high academic achievement will make them less popular with their peers. Teenagers who get good grades at school sometimes encounter teasing, name-calling, and exclusion from groups. Faced with these negative reactions, teens who want to do well sometimes decide to study in secret, resulting in a lot of extra stress.

Peer pressure

By the time they enter their teens, most young people are spending less time with their families and more time with their peers. Teenagers' willingness to conform to their parents' expectations lessens as their need for privacy and acceptance by their peers increases. Greater independence can be exciting, but it can be stressful, too. **Peer pressure** is particularly strong during the high school years.

Many young people experience pressure from their peers to do things they don't really want to do. They may be pushed to try out new experiences, such as smoking, taking illegal drugs, drinking alcohol, or engaging in sexual activities.

Some students give in to peer pressure because they want to fit in. They fear that refusal will cause them to lose friends and be unpopular. Other teens, however, decide to take a stand and say no. Sometimes their position is respected; occasionally they end up feeling lonely and misunderstood. In either situation, teenagers are in danger of becoming depressed as they

Friends can put teens in a difficult situation by pressuring them to do things that feel wrong.

struggle alone with difficult situations and decisions. They need a trusted adult to talk to for advice and support.

Being left out

Some teenagers have to cope with cruel treatment from their peers and are deliberately excluded from groups or cliques. Teens sometimes pick on peers who are thought of as "different" because of their skin color, their weight, or a physical or mental disability. Cruel treatment can cause serious emotional consequences. Excluded teenagers may experience loneliness, humiliation, and despair, as well as pent-up frustration and rage. Being excluded can also interfere with a student's interest and ability to learn in school.

Being excluded from social groups can leave teens feeling lonely and unhappy. This experience can be a factor in depression.

Teens who are bullied can feel that there is no escape.

Bullying

Bullying is one of the hardest things a teenager may have to face. It can take many forms, but it is always mean and frightening. Every day, about 160,000 kids miss school because of bullying and school violence.

Bullies use a number of different methods, such as abusive phone calls, threatening text messages, and embarrassing or insulting comments on Internet sites or in e-mails. A bully may focus on a specific characteristic of his or her victim— appearance, voice, race, religion, or sexuality, for example. Bullies usually mock their targets and call them insulting names. They may threaten or carry out violence and steal or damage others' possessions. Sometimes bullies spread rumors about other people.

Bullying can have long-term psychological effects on both bullies and their victims. Bullying behavior has been linked to other forms of destructive behavior, such as skipping school, shoplifting, fighting, and drug and alcohol abuse. Victims of bullying can experience loneliness, fear, humiliation, loss of self-esteem, frustration, rage, and even thoughts of suicide. The damage caused by bullying can last into adulthood.

In focus: *violence in schools*

Students are less likely to be victims of a violent crime at school than in other settings. However, any instance of crime or violence at school can have lasting effects, including depression. In recent years, a very high percentage of middle schools and high schools reported incidents of crime and violence, according to the National Center for Education Statistics. Although most acts of school violence are minor assaults, some episodes are far more serious and end in tragedy.

The presence of weapons at school creates an intimidating and threatening atmosphere. In 2005, about 8 percent of U.S. students reported being threatened or injured with a weapon, such as a gun or a knife, at school. Every month, almost a million students bring a weapon to school. Many teenagers today report a sense of anxiety because they do not feel safe at school. Some schools have responded by installing metal detectors, adding security officers, and adopting zero-tolerance policies for students who bring weapons onto school property. School officials have also introduced counseling and conflict-resolution programs and emphasized better communication between school and home.

CASE STUDY

When Amit was 12 years old, he started at a new school, but he found it very hard to fit in. All the other boys stuck together and made him feel left out. Some of the students told him he wasn't wanted and made fun of him because of the way he spoke and dressed. The bullies also sent him threatening text messages and posted cruel comments on the Internet.

Amit felt trapped and afraid. Some of the bullies had warned him that they would "get him" if he ever reported them to his parents or to school officials, so Amit kept his misery to himself. He stayed home from school as often as he could and spent a lot of time alone. He thought a lot about the cruel remarks and actions of his peers. Amit started to believe all the terrible things the bullies had said about him. He was overcome by negative thoughts and decided that there was no hope for the future. When Amit's dad found the boy trying to cut his wrists, the father realized that his son had a serious problem. Amit was severely depressed and suicidal.

Changing bodies

As girls and boys enter **puberty**, their bodies start to change and develop. These years can be difficult, and many young people have trouble coping with the physical changes.

Girls often feel self-conscious about their new shape, especially if they develop earlier than their friends do. Boys may feel embarrassed when their voices begin to break. Meanwhile, youngsters who start puberty late can feel awkward that their bodies have not yet developed. These factors can cause some teenagers to withdraw and become depressed.

About eight in 10 preteens and teens have acne, a condition that can cause skin breakouts. Acne can be particularly upsetting for young people and can make them avoid social events and settings. Teens who have severe acne may experience a loss of self-confidence and self-esteem. A Canadian research study found that even a mild case of acne can bring on depression and thoughts of suicide.

As teenagers enter puberty, they have to cope with many changes. They must get used to their changing bodies and adjust to the pressures of relating to the opposite sex.

Sexual pressures

As teenagers develop adult bodies, they start to have sexual feelings. At the same time, they start to attract the attention of the opposite sex. For some teenagers, this sexual attention feels very threatening, and they may withdraw into depression.

When teenagers start to "go out" with the opposite sex, a new element of competition can enter their friendships. For example, if two girls compete for the attention of the same boy, their friendship may become strained. Some teens who are not yet dating can feel left out by friends who are couples. Other teenagers may worry that they are not "normal" if they don't have a romantic relationship by a certain age.

During the middle school and high school years, young people may experience stress because of romantic feelings and relationships.

In focus: pressure to be thin

As girls reach puberty, they start to gain weight and develop some natural curves. At the same time, however, they may feel intense pressure to be slim. Wherever they look—in magazines and movies or on TV—they see super-thin models and celebrities and read advice on dieting. Some teenagers respond to the pressure by becoming very unhappy about the way their bodies look. Their self-esteem drops sharply, and some teens even develop eating disorders, such as anorexia and bulimia. (See Chapter 1.)

Chapter 3: *At risk*

Most experts believe that depression is caused by a combination of physical, **psychological**, and environmental factors. Certain characteristics or events can put some people at greater risk than others. However, it is important to note that belonging to a high-risk group doesn't necessarily mean that a person will develop depression.

Families under pressure

Some teenagers have to cope with extreme pressures at home. If their parents have an **addiction** to alcohol or other drugs, children may live with high levels of fear and anxiety. Over time, these feelings can develop into a sense of deep depression and helplessness.

In families where a parent has a serious illness, injury, or disability, children often must take on many extra responsibilities. In some cases, the children become their parents' caregivers and spend much of their time at home. These teens miss out on social activities and sometimes even skip school. Teenagers faced with this sort of pressure can become lonely and discouraged.

Violence, abuse, and neglect

For some children, home is not a safe place. Their parents may treat them or other family members violently. Young people may experience **physical abuse** or **sexual abuse** from other family members or family friends. Some children are

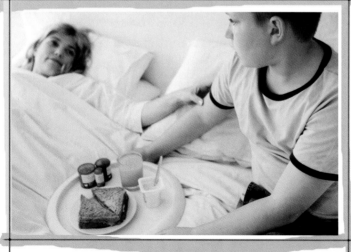

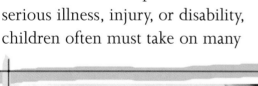

When children have to take on the role of caregiver, they can become overwhelmed by worry and feelings of helplessness.

CASE STUDY

Whenever friends asked Rick to play football after school, he always said no. He never gave a reason. None of his friends knew that Rick had to rush home to look after his mom. Rick's mother had a disability, and he had been her main caregiver since he was 12 years old. She relied on him to shop, cook meals, clean the home, and help her get into and out of bed.

Rick often felt worried and burdened by the responsibility. He also felt sad and angry because he thought his friends wouldn't understand what he was going through. After a while, the other boys stopped asking Rick to do things with them. He began to stay home from school more often. Even though he loved his mother, a future spent caring for her seemed very bleak to him. Sometimes he felt so depressed that he could hardly find the strength to get out of bed.

neglected and lack basic necessities, such as adequate food and clothing. All these experiences are deeply distressing and frightening and can cause lasting emotional damage.

Teenagers who are faced with serious problems, such as violence in the home, should never have to cope alone. There are many organizations and people to whom they can turn for help. (See page 47 for a list of helplines and web sites.)

If teenagers try to cope with problems on their own, they can end up feeling severely depressed and even suicidal.

Some teenagers experience violence in their homes or their personal relationships. In these frightening situations, teens often become withdrawn and depressed.

Stressful events

In addition to all the usual stresses of growing up, some teenagers have to cope with major causes of distress. Certain events, such as the death of a family member, a friend, or a classmate, can cause overwhelming feelings of grief and helplessness. The death of a beloved pet can also leave a teenager feeling lonely and sad.

Many young people experience depression after their parents have separated or divorced. It is common for teenagers to become depressed when they have to change homes and leave their old friends behind.

Some teens become depressed following a breakup with a boyfriend or girlfriend. Ending a relationship or being "dumped" is never easy,

Some teens become depressed as they struggle to cope with terrible tragedies. In many cases, they need expert support and counseling to help them recover.

especially when the circumstances are widely known among a group of friends.

Many young people are able to cope with the stresses of negative life events and move on. But for others, who may be especially susceptible to depression, the events pile up and the stresses are too great. In these teens, traumatic events may trigger depression.

Talking about one's problems can be a great relief. Sometimes, just discussing a situation calmly helps teens cope more effectively with their feelings.

CASE STUDY

After going out for six months, Sonia and Joe broke up. Sonia's family and friends thought she'd soon get over her sadness about the breakup. Three weeks later, however, she was still staying in bed for most of the day. Sonia spent most of the time sleeping or watching TV. She also stopped caring about her appearance and refused invitations to go out with her friends. Her mother recognized the signs of depression and arranged for Sonia to see a psychotherapist.

Over the next few weeks, Sonia talked with the therapist about the things that were troubling her. Sonia said she was still sad about her parents' divorce, which had occurred four years earlier. Sonia was also worried that she might fail at school. While she was going out with Joe, she had managed to push those concerns to the back of her mind, but now they were overwhelming her.

With the help of the therapist, Sonia talked about her feelings and worries and grew to understand them better. After a few months, she felt better able to cope with her concerns. She began to enjoy life with her family and friends once again.

Some teens deal with feelings of sadness by going on shopping sprees. Sadly, this often makes their problems worse because they have to cope with money problems, too.

Teenagers in trouble

It is not unusual for young people to get into some sort of trouble during their teenage years. Issues can range from difficulties at school to more serious problems such as criminal offenses.

Some teenagers may engage in deliberately risky behavior—driving recklessly or "car surfing," for example. Young people also take risks by having unprotected sex. This behavior increases the risk of contracting sexually transmitted diseases.

Debt stress

Some young people experience money problems and get into debt. Teenagers spent about $180 billion in 2006, according to Teenage Research Unlimited, a company that tracks teen spending. A U.S. financial services company found that almost one-third of teens admit owing money. One out of seven teens says his or her debt exceeds $1,000.

Gambling is on the rise among teenagers, and Internet gambling is an especially serious problem. A growing number of teens have gotten hooked on the excitement of games like Internet poker and then found themselves in serious debt. Researchers say that teen gamblers are more likely to report depression than teenagers who did not gamble.

Faced with the anxiety of being in debt, teens can become depressed.

They need help to cope with their situation and take charge of their lives.

Drugs and alcohol

Some young people experiment with alcohol and drugs. Those substances are frequently associated with depression. A recent U.S. study found that 12- to 17-year-olds with depression were about twice as likely to start abusing alcohol or drugs as teenagers who had not experienced depression over the past year. Researchers are not sure whether anxiety and depression lead to alcohol and drug abuse or whether using alcohol and drugs leads to depression.

Teenagers who become addicted to alcohol or drugs can experience a tragic downward spiral that may lead to severe depression and even suicide. Young people who reported using alcohol or drugs were more likely than non-abusers to be at risk of attempting suicide.

Depressed teens who abuse drugs or alcohol need professional support to overcome their problems. Yet experts estimate that only 40 percent of young people at risk for suicide receive mental health treatment or counseling.

The effects of diet

In some cases, diet can be a factor in causing depression. When teenagers

It's a fact: marijuana linked with depression

Some people claim that the use of marijuana has no serious side effects. Medical researchers warn, however, that frequent marijuana use may trigger depression, especially among girls. Doctors who surveyed 1,600 teenage girls in Australia over a period of seven years published these findings:

- Girls who used the drug daily were five times as likely to become depressed and experience anxiety as girls who did not use marijuana.

- Girls who used marijuana at least once a week were twice as likely as nonusers to develop depression.

eat a diet that is high in sugar and fat, they may soon become exhausted, have headaches, and feel miserable. **Allergies** to certain foods, such as wheat and dairy products, can also have a powerful effect on mood, making people feel very low.

Girls at risk

Statistics show that girls are twice as likely as boys to develop depression in their teenage years. Experts have offered a number of reasons that girls develop depression more frequently than boys. Some research indicates that girls are more likely than boys to have difficulties accepting the physical changes of puberty. Many teenage girls become extremely self-critical, and low self-esteem can contribute to

depression. Changing levels of female hormones can trigger mood swings.

Studies have shown that teenage girls are more socially oriented than boys. Girls are more likely to develop close relationships, and they are also more vulnerable to depression when relationships end.

In some families, and in society in general, expectations of behavior are different for boys and girls. Boys are often encouraged to be more assertive than girls. Faced with this double standard, some girls **internalize** their negative feelings, keeping their anger and frustration tightly under control. Eventually, these feelings can lead to depression.

Studies have shown that teenage girls and boys tend to have different ways of coping with stressful events. It is common for boys to "act out" or to find a way to distract themselves from their problems. Some experts say that girls tend to dwell on their

Depression is much more common among girls than among boys. One possible factor for the different rates is girls' tendency to worry more about schoolwork and exams.

difficulties and can end up feeling helpless and depressed.

A family problem?

Medical researchers have found evidence that a tendency to become depressed can be inherited. However, it is hard to know exactly what role inheritance plays in depression. If a child with a depressed parent develops depression, is it the result of a family tendency? Or is it a reaction to a difficult situation at home as the child watches the parent struggling to cope? Most experts agree that although family history can play a part in the development of depression, the illness is the result of many factors.

Children who live for many years with a depressed parent are at risk of experiencing depression when they are older. However, not all children who have depressed parents go on to develop depression themselves.

In focus: high-risk personalities

Some personality types are especially vulnerable to depression. Young people with low self-esteem can feel a sense of overwhelming despair when they are faced with difficulties. Teenagers who are **introverted** and tend to keep their problems to themselves run a higher risk of becoming depressed than more **extroverted** teens do. Another vulnerable group includes **perfectionists**, who often set unrealistic goals for themselves. If they fail to meet their goals, they may blame themselves bitterly and feel distressed and demoralized.

Chapter 4: *Getting help*

Many teenagers with depression make a full recovery, but they need expert help and the support of family members and friends. Fortunately, experienced mental health professionals are available to help.

Taking the first step to wellness

The first step on the road to recovery is finding someone to talk to. Some teenagers decide to share their feelings with a parent, another family member, or a close friend. Others prefer to talk to a school counselor or a doctor. Some young people use the Internet or call a telephone helpline to find a counselor who can help them with their problems.

Simply having someone to share thoughts and feelings with can make a person

Making the decision to call a helpline can be an important step toward recovery.

with depression feel much better. For some people with mild depression, talking with a trusted adult can help them emerge from their illness. Many others, however, need professional help to recover.

Individual therapy

Most people with depression can be greatly helped by a course of counseling or psychotherapy. Regular sessions may continue for weeks or months, depending on the severity of the patient's depression. During the sessions, patients are encouraged to explore the reasons underlying their depression. They are also helped to cope with their negative feelings.

Expert counseling can help teenagers understand why they feel depressed. Therapy can also point the way to making positive changes so that teens no longer feel overwhelmed by their difficulties. Counseling often helps people recognize and change behaviors that might have contributed to their depression. For example, some depressed teens blame themselves for events or situations that are not their fault.

Counselors can help young people who are depressed develop strategies to cope with stress. Counselors can also teach people how to be more aware of the events, situations, and thoughts that trigger their negative feelings. Then teenagers can take steps to avoid those situations in the future.

Most professional counselors keep conversations confidential unless a young person is in danger. Then, the counselor must involve other people and agencies, such as the patient's parents and the police.

It's a fact:
treatment for depression

- Research has found that only about one-third of teenagers with depression receive mental health treatment.
- The consequences of untreated teenage depression can include severe depression in adult life as well as problems with crime and substance abuse.
- Researchers for the National Institute of Mental Health found that as many as 7 percent of depressed teens may commit suicide as young adults.

Family and group therapy

When a teenager becomes depressed, it can be helpful to bring the family together for therapy. **Family therapy** enables the family members to explore conflicts and tensions in a safe environment. A therapist can help parents and their teenage children understand one another's point of view and find better ways to interact.

Sometimes a small group of people with similar problems attend therapy sessions together. **Group therapy** gives patients the opportunity to compare their thoughts and feelings and to support one another in their efforts to get well.

Medication

Sometimes doctors decide that a course of treatment should include medication as well as therapy. A **psychiatrist** or another doctor may prescribe an **antidepressant** to help lift a patient's mood and maximize the benefits from therapy.

Talking to others with similar problems can help in young people's recovery from depression.

Sometimes therapists bring parents and children together to discuss their problems. Family therapy can be a positive way of dealing with conflict.

In focus: antidepressants and young patients

Some medical professionals and others have recently raised concerns about an increased risk of suicidal thoughts and behavior in children and teens taking antidepressants. As a result, the U.S. Food and Drug Administration requires a printed warning on the label of all antidepressants about their use by people up to the age of 24.

Children and teens being treated with antidepressants should be closely observed for any increase in agitation, irritability, suicidal thoughts, and unusual changes in behavior. Observation for these changes is especially important during the initial few months of drug therapy or at times of dose changes, either increases or decreases. As young people approach the end of their treatment, they need to decrease their daily dose of drugs in gradual steps. That enables them to avoid withdrawal reactions such as **nausea**, dizziness, and sleep difficulties.

Having supportive friends can make a big difference in recovery from depression.

Once someone has started treatment for depression, it's very important to persist, even though it can seem hard at times. Attending regular therapy sessions and carefully following a doctor's instructions can help people make good progress toward recovery.

Keeping a journal

Keeping a daily journal of thoughts and feelings can be a great help in achieving recovery. A daily record helps people recognize and understand what triggers their depression or lifts their mood. It allows them to express their feelings rather than struggling with buried emotions. A journal can also help therapists as they work with depressed teens.

Finding a support system

When teenagers are recovering from depression, they need plenty of help and support. There will still be times when they feel down, and it is important that they have understanding people with whom they can talk. These people may be friends, parents, mental health professionals, or peer counselors at a helpline. The most important thing is that they are supportive, reassuring, and compassionate.

For some teens, support groups play a valuable role in recovery. These groups are made up of people who have experienced depression and recovered.

Eating well

The things people eat and drink can have a powerful effect on their mood. In particular, research has shown that food that is rich in B vitamins can improve mood and may reduce the risk of developing depression. Orange juice, strawberries, leafy green vegetables, and whole-grain breads are good sources of vitamin B. Some doctors recommend daily multivitamin and mineral supplements.

Sleeping well

Sleeping well can help young people recover from depression. Being rested enables them to better cope with stress. Doctors advise teens to follow a routine, going to bed and getting up at roughly the same time every day.

Keeping a journal can help young people keep in touch with their feelings and "let off steam."

Chapter 5: *Coping with stress*

All people have to deal with stress in their lives, and there are times when the pressures feel overwhelming. Stress doesn't have to win the battle, though. There are ways of coping that can help young people avoid depression.

Looking after yourself

When you feel anxious and overstressed, it's tempting to hide away from the world. In fact, withdrawing from others will make you feel worse. If you follow a few simple tips for taking care of yourself, you will be better able to deal with the stresses of everyday life.

Looking after yourself is really just common sense. You need to make sure you get enough sleep and exercise. Take time to eat breakfast in the morning, and eat balanced, nutritious meals throughout the day. Wearing clean clothes and showering daily also boost your self-esteem. When you make the effort to get out with friends and do things you enjoy, you will discover that you feel more positive about your life.

Staying aware

It's important to recognize when you are feeling stressed or falling into destructive patterns of behavior. If you sense that you are becoming overly anxious, make a deliberate effort to slow down and relax. Find some time in your day for reflection. You might choose to take a warm bath, practice yoga, or go outdoors for a walk. Reading a favorite book or listening to soothing music can be relaxing. You could also get together with friends for an activity that you enjoy.

Getting help

If you feel that pressures at home or at school are getting the better of you, don't keep your worries to yourself. Feeling depressed is nothing to be ashamed of, and you should never feel that you have to deal with depression on your own. There are plenty of people who will understand what you are going through and who can help you feel better.

Start by talking to someone in your family or to another adult you trust. You can also check out the contacts listed on page 47 of this book.

In focus: *beating stress*

Here are some ideas for keeping your life as stress-free as possible.

- Take some time out every day to relax and do something you enjoy.
- Cut down on sugary foods, cola, and coffee. They can make you feel "wired" and stressed.
- Avoid cigarettes. Although smoking may seem to relieve stress in the short term, feelings of anxiety will quickly return.
- Laugh. Watch a funny film, tell a joke, or read a comic.
- Get plenty of sleep, fresh air, and exercise.
- Remove clutter from your life. Organize your room, and throw away unimportant papers on your desk.
- Make a list of all the demands on your time and energy for one week. Give priority to the most important tasks, and do those first.
- Break up big projects into smaller, more manageable tasks so that you do not feel overwhelmed.
- Set realistic expectations and deadlines for yourself.
- Putting off tasks adds to feelings of stress. Don't delay doing homework or studying for exams.
- Do not keep worries to yourself. Talk them over with a friend.
- Write about your feelings in a journal. Keeping a diary can help make you more aware of the sorts of things that make you feel stressed.

One of the best ways to avoid depression is to get plenty of exercise, The best activities involve having fun with friends!

45

Glossary

addiction: compulsive need for and use of a habit-forming substance

allergies: physical reactions (such as sneezing, breathing problems, or itching) to a substance

anorexia nervosa: an eating disorder in which people feel an extreme need to be thin. They have a distorted body image, abnormal eating patterns, malnutrition, and excessive weight loss.

antidepressant: a medication taken to treat depression by altering the balance of chemicals in the brain

anxiety: an extreme feeling of worry or fear

binge: to eat a very large amount of food in a short time

bipolar disorder: a mental illness in which periods of depression alternate with periods of feeling overly excited

bulimia nervosa: an eating disorder in which people binge on large amounts of food and then try to empty their bodies of the food by purging, usually through vomiting or taking laxatives

compulsive eating disorder: an eating disorder in which people feel an overwhelming need to keep eating even when they are full

counselors: people who are trained to provide support and advice

depression: a mood disorder marked by persistent sadness, inactivity, difficulty in concentration, a significant increase or decrease in appetite and sleep, and feelings of hopelessness

eating disorder: an eating problem such as anorexia nervosa, bulimia nervosa, binge-eating disorder, or compulsive eating disorder

extroverted: outgoing and apparently confident

family therapy: counseling that involves the patient and one or more members of his or her family

fatigue: tiredness or exhaustion from stress

group therapy: counseling that involves two or more people with the same problem

insomnia: difficulties in sleeping

internalize: to keep something hidden within

introverted: shy and not outgoing

laxatives: substances that cause people to expel solid wastes from the body

lithium: a medication that prevents people from experiencing extreme highs and lows in mood

manic: overly excited

mental illness: a disorder that affects thinking and behavior

nausea: stomach distress with an urge to vomit

peer pressure: pressure from people of the same age and in the same situation

perfectionists: people who seek or demand perfection, usually to an unreasonable degree

physical abuse: physical mistreatment of one person by another

psychiatrist: a medical doctor who treats people with mental illness and who can prescribe medication

psychological: relating to the mind and the emotions

psychotherapy: the process of helping someone with emotional or mental health problems, mainly through talking with them

puberty: a series of physical changes that marks the end of childhood and the start of sexual maturity

purge: to get rid of food from the body, usually by vomiting or taking laxatives

seasonal affective disorder (SAD): a mental health problem in which people respond to a lack of sunlight by becoming depressed

self-esteem: positive feelings about oneself

self-harm: actions, such as cutting or burning, by which people deliberately hurt themselves

sexual abuse: physical or sexual contact with a person against his or her will

stress: mental tension resulting from factors that cause strain or pressure

Further information

Books to read

Cobain, Bev. *When Nothing Matters Anymore: Survival Guide of Depressed Teens* (rev. ed.). Minneapolis, Minn.: Free Spirit Publishing, 2007.

Piquemal, Michael, Oliver Tossan, and Melissa Daly. *When Life Stinks: How to Deal with Your Bad Moods and Depression.* New York: Harry N. Abrams, 2004.

Schab, Lisa. *Beyond the Blues: A Workbook to Help Teens Overcome Depression.* Oakland, Calif.: Instant Help Books, 2008.

Vizzini, Ned. *It's Kind of a Funny Story.* New York: Miramax Books, 2006.

Winkler, Kathleen. *Teens, Depression, and the Blues: A Hot Issue* (Hot Issues). Berkeley Heights, N.J.: Enslow Publishers, 2000.

Organizations to contact

National Suicide Prevention Lifeline
Web site: **www.suicidepreventionlifeline.org**
Toll-free helpline: 1-800-273-TALK (8255)
The National Suicide Prevention Lifeline is a 24-hour suicide prevention service that provides immediate, confidential assistance to people in crisis. Callers are connected to the nearest available suicide prevention and mental health service provider.

National Alliance on Mental Illness (NAMI)
Web site: **www.nami.org**
Toll-free helpline: 1-800-950-NAMI (6264)
NAMI provides information, referral, and education on mental health problems. The helpline is available Monday through Friday, 10 A.M. to 6 P.M. Eastern time.

Helpful web sites

HealthyPlace.com Depression Community
www.healthyplace.com/Communities/ Depression/children.asp
This web site provides statistics and information about depression and its causes, symptoms, and treatment options.

Helpguide: Dealing With Teen Depression
www.helpguide.org/mental/depression_ teen_teenagers.htm
The Helpguide article "Tips and Tools for Helping Yourself or a Friend" includes information on signs and symptoms of depression; dealing with thoughts of suicide; strategies for feeling better; talking to parents about depression; and helping a depressed friend.

National Institute of Mental Health (NIMH)
www.nimh.nih.gov/health/topics/ depression/index.shtml
NIMH is the world's largest scientific organization aimed at researching the promotion of mental health and the treatment of mental disorders.

TeensHealth
kidshealth.org/teen/your_mind/ mental_health/depression.html and **kidshealth.org/teen/your_mind/ emotions/stress.html**
TeensHealth (part of the KidsHealth web site) provides teenagers and families with accurate, up-to-date content developed by physicians and other health experts.

Publisher's note to educators and parents: Our editors have carefully reviewed these web sites to ensure that they are suitable for children. Many web sites change frequently, however, and we cannot guarantee that a site's future contents will continue to meet our high standards of quality and educational value. Be advised that children should be closely supervised whenever they access the Internet.

Index